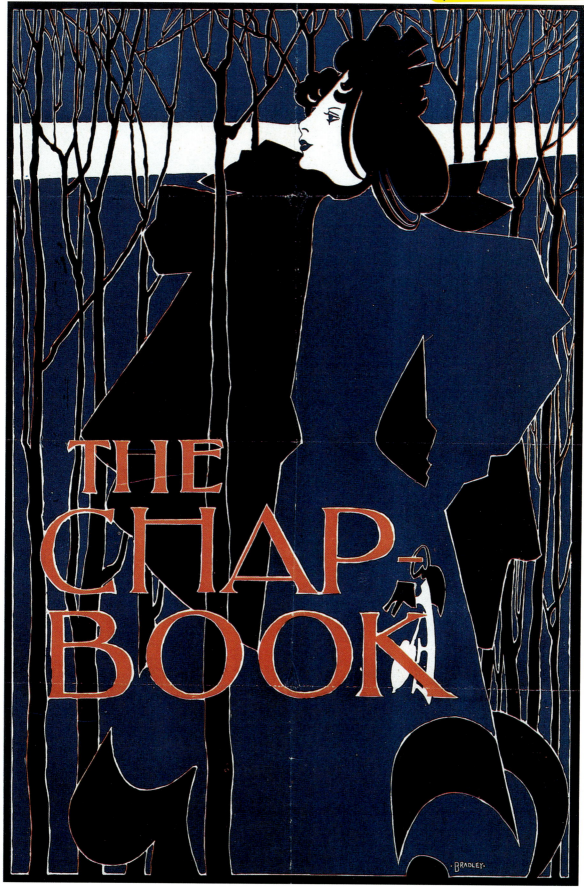

001. WILLIAM H. BRADLEY (1868–1962)
Blue Lady, "The Chap-Book," 1894
18½ x 12½ in. (46.5 x 31.6 cm)

002. WILLIAM H. BRADLEY (1868–1962)
When Hearts are Trumps, 1894
16¼ x 13½ in. (41.7 x 34.1 cm)

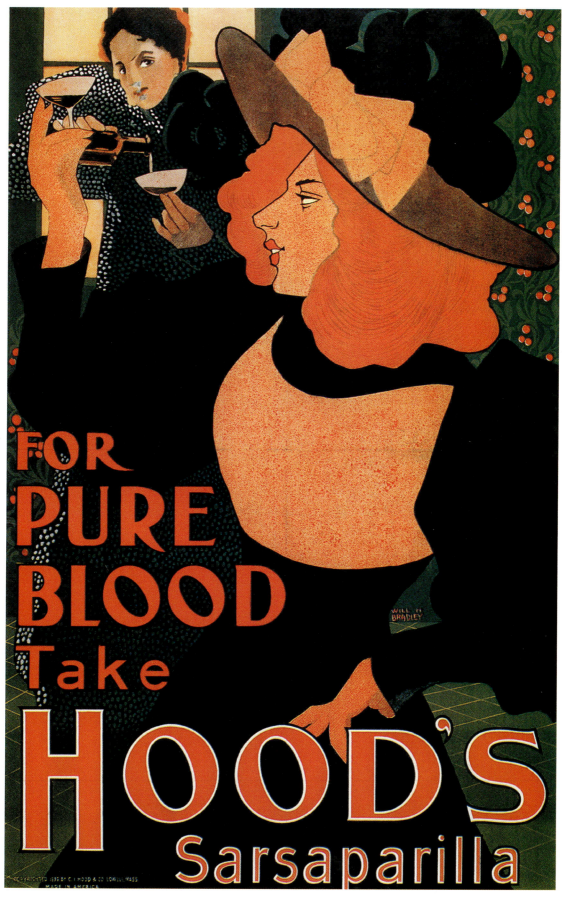

003. WILLIAM H. BRADLEY (1868–1962)
Hood's Sarsaparilla, 1896
27⅛ x 40⅞ in. (69 x 104 cm)

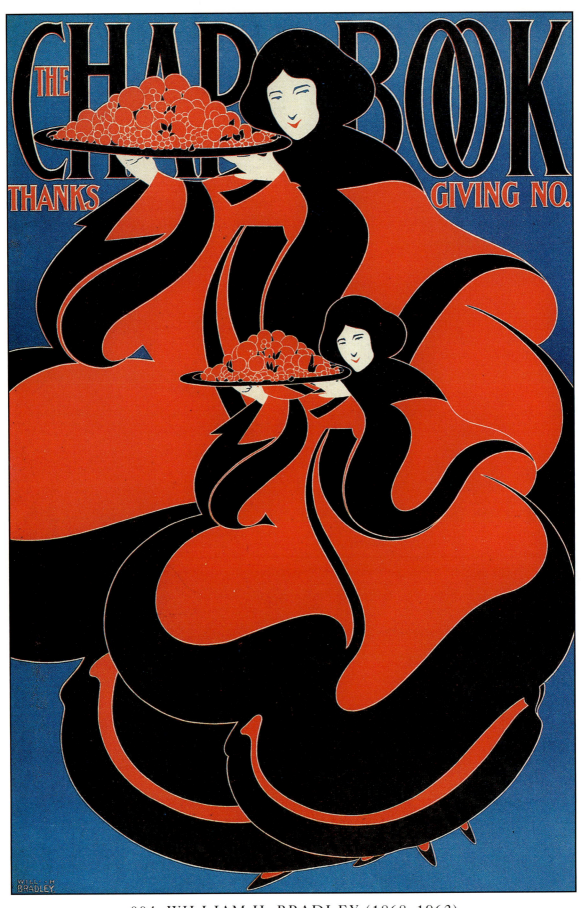

004. WILLIAM H. BRADLEY (1868–1962)
Thanksgiving Number, "The Chap-Book," 1895
19⅝ x 18⅞ in. (49.9 x 33.8 cm)

005. WILLIAM H. BRADLEY (1868–1962)
May, "The Chap-Book," 1895
20⅛ x 13¼ in. (51 x 33.8 cm)

VICTOR BICYCLES

OVERMAN WHEEL CO.

Boston • New York • Detroit • Denver •
San Francisco • Los Angeles • Portland ore.

006. WILLIAM H. BRADLEY (1868–1962)
Victor Bicycles, Overman Wheel Co., 1896
27 x 40¾ in. (68.5 x 104.2 cm)

007. WILLIAM H. BRADLEY (1868–1962)
The Inland Printer, Christmas, 1895
17½ x 14 in. (44 x 36 cm)

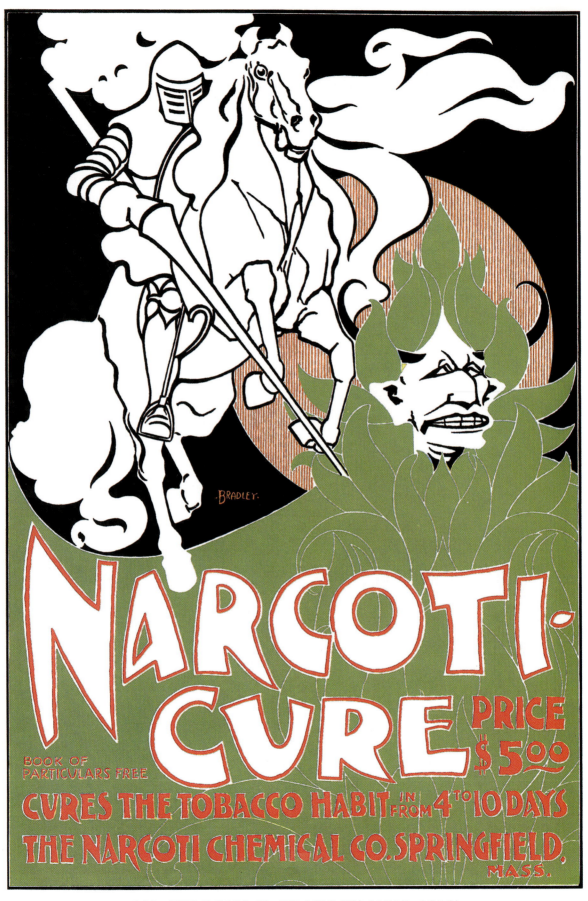

008. WILLIAM H. BRADLEY (1868–1962)
Narcoti-Cure, 1895
20 x 13½ in. (50 x 34 cm)

009. WILLIAM H. BRADLEY (1868–1962)
The Kiss, "Bradley: His Book," 1896
39⅞ x 27 in. (101.3 x 68.6 cm)

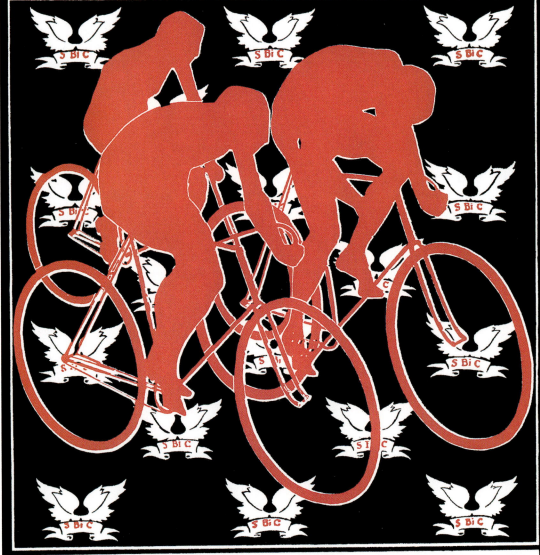

010. WILLIAM H. BRADLEY (1868–1962)
Springfield Bicycle Club Tournament, 1895
14 x 21 in. (36 x 53 cm)

011. WILLIAM H. BRADLEY (1868–1962)
Christmas, "Bradley: His Book," 1896
39½ x 26⅝ in. (100.7 x 67.7 cm)

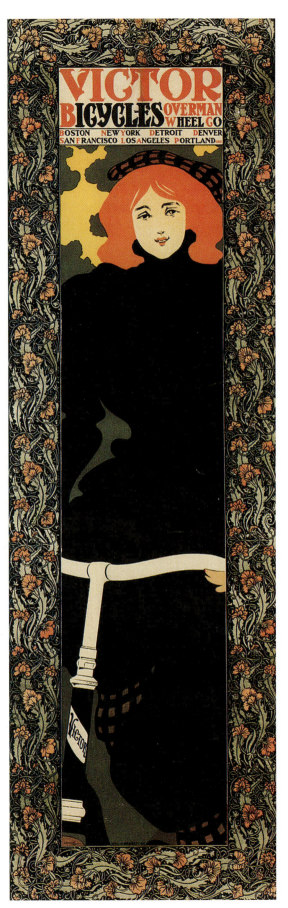

012. WILLIAM H. BRADLEY (1868–1962)
Victor Bicycles, Overman Wheel Co., 1895
40⅛ x 12⅞ in. (102.1 x 32.6 cm)

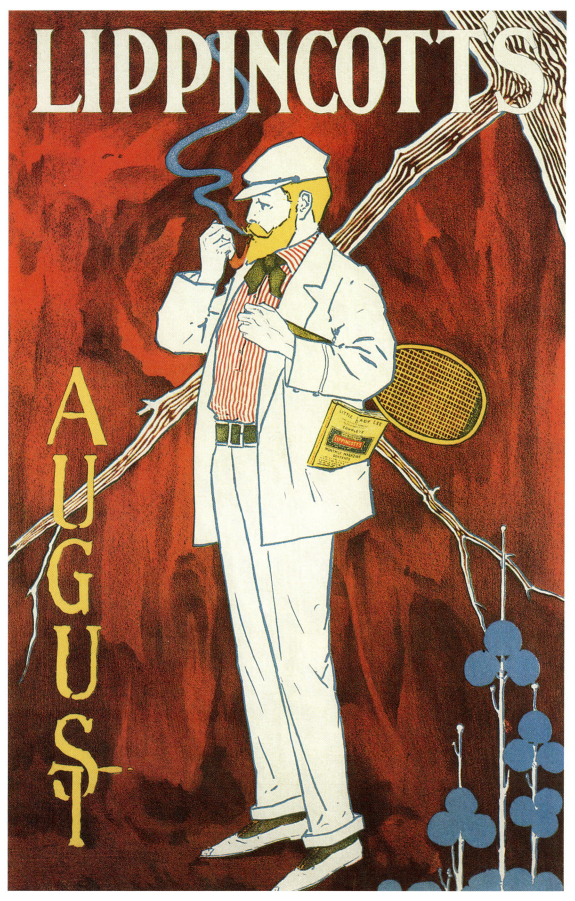

013. WILLIAM L. CARQUEVILLE (1871–1946)
Lippincott's August, 1895
18½ x 12⅛ in. (46.9 x 30.7 cm)

014. WILLIAM L. CARQUEVILLE (1871–1946)
Lippincott's February, 1895
19⅛ x 12⅝ in. (48.4 x 32.1 cm)

015. WILLIAM L. CARQUEVILLE (1871–1946)
Lippincott's May, 1895
19 x 12½ in. (48 x 31.5 cm)

016. WILLIAM L. CARQUEVILLE (1871–1946)
Lippincott's January, 1895
18⅞ x 12 in. (48 x 31.7 cm)

017. CHARLES ARTHUR COX (1829–1901)
Bearings, ca. 1896
18 x 13¼ in. (45.7 x 33.6 cm)

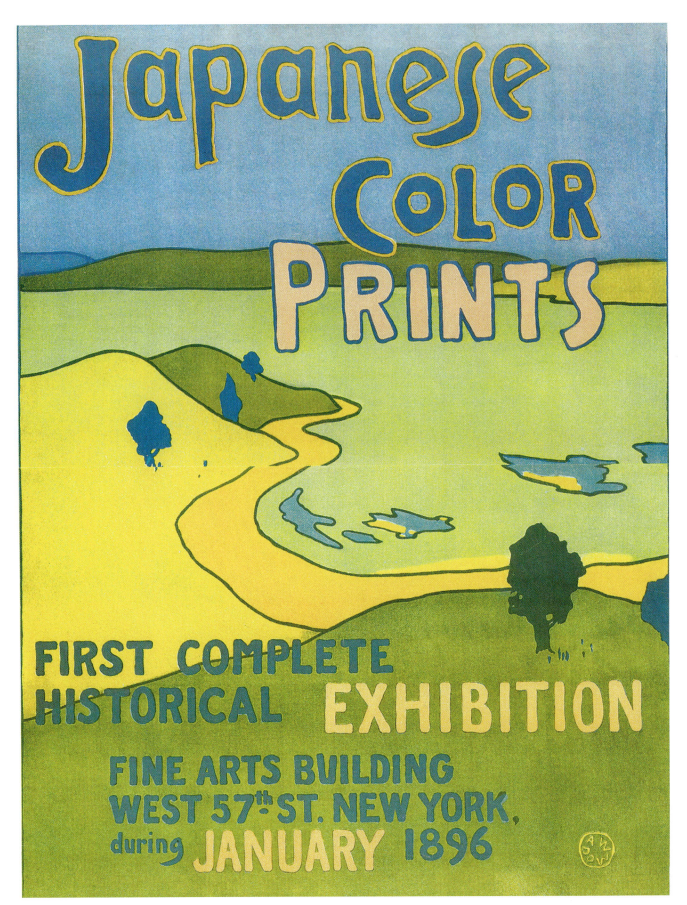

018. ARTHUR WESLEY DOW (1857–1922)
Japanese Color Prints, 1896

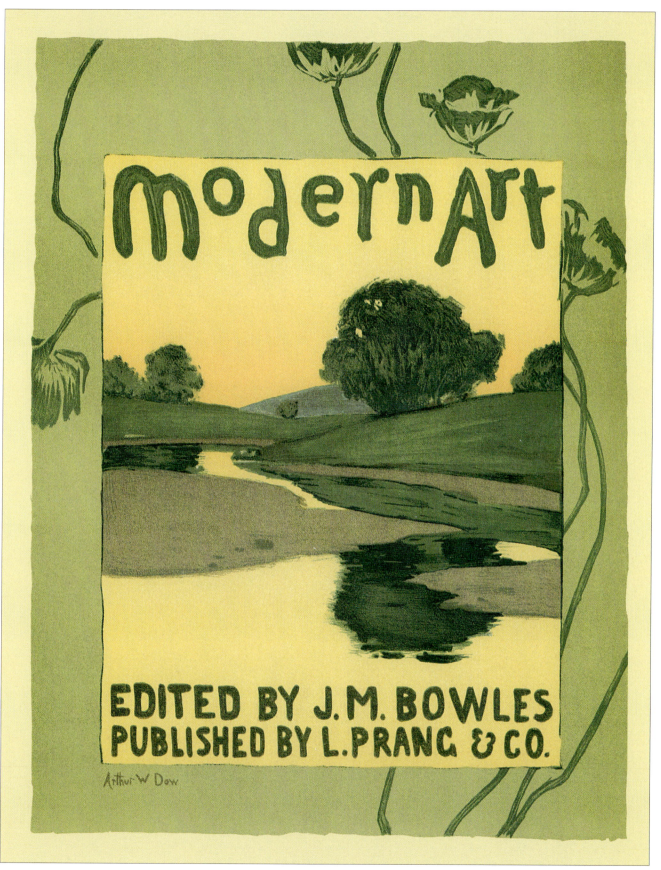

019. ARTHUR WESLEY DOW (1857–1922)
Modern Art, 1895
21 x 15½ in. (54 x 39 cm)

020. ALICE RUSSELL GLENNY (1858–1924)
Womens Edition (Buffalo) Courier, 1895
24¼ x 14⅛ in. (61.7 x 37 cm)

021. JOSEPH J. GOULD, JR. (1880–1935)
Lippincott's December, 1896
15½ x 12⅞ in. (39.6 x 32.8 cm)

022. FRANK HAZENPLUG (1873–1931)
Red Lady, "The Chap-Book," 1895
13⅜ x 7⅞ in. (34 x 20.1 cm)

023. JOSEPH CHRISTIAN LEYENDECKER (1874–1951)
The Century Midsummer Holiday Number, August, 1896
15 x 14⅛ in. (38.2 x 35.5 cm)

024. WILL HICOK LOW (1853–1932)
Scribner's Fiction Number, ca. 1895
19½ x 13¼ in. (49.5 x 33.6 cm)

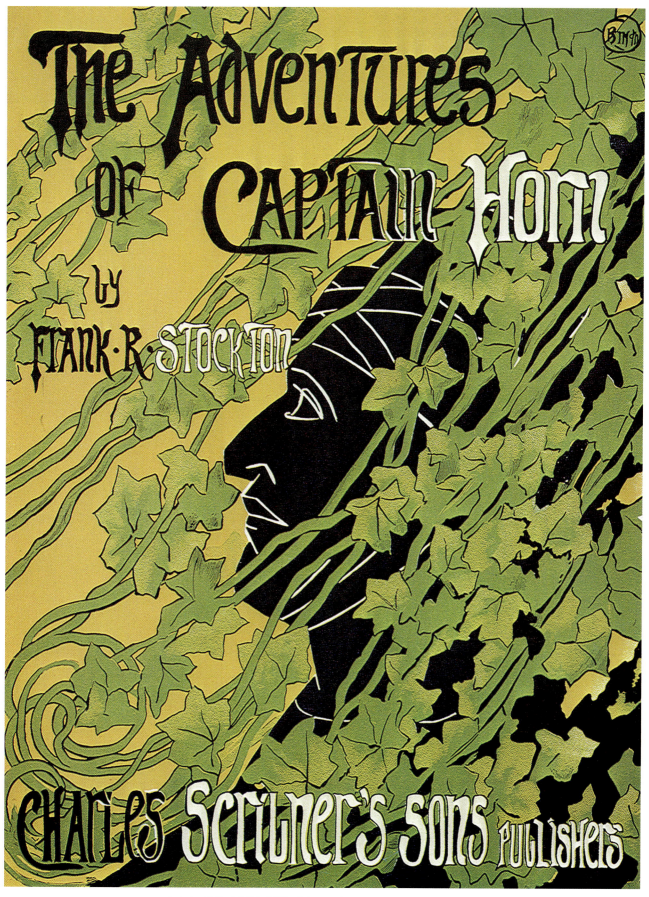

025. BLANCHE McMANUS (1870–1929)
The Adventures of Captain Horn, 1895
16⅛ x 12 in. (41.2 x 30.5 cm)

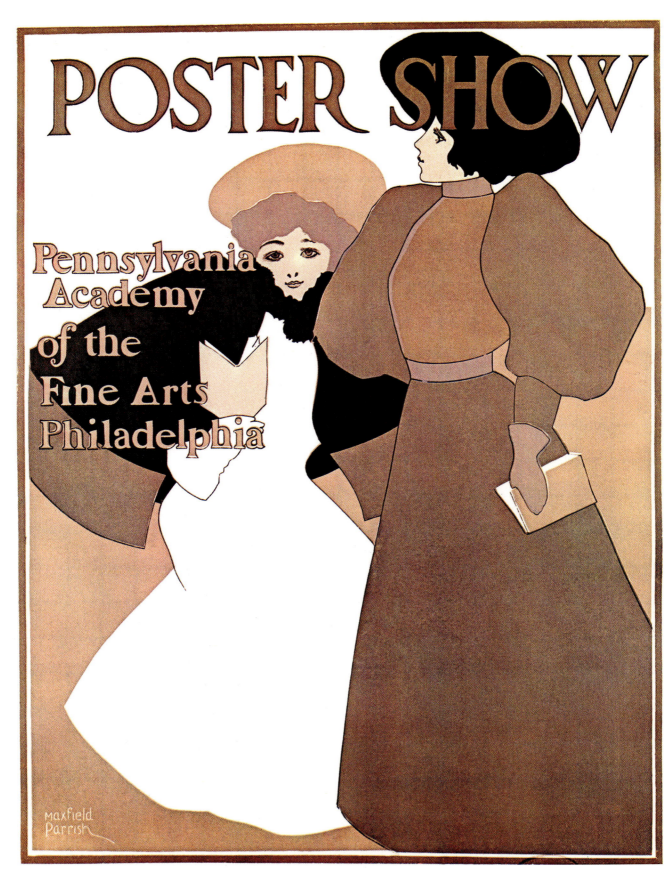

026. MAXFIELD PARRISH (1870–1966)
Poster Show, 1896
44 x 28 in. (111.7 x 71.1 cm)

027. MAXFIELD PARRISH (1870–1966)
The Century, 1897
20 x 13½ in. (51 x 34 cm)

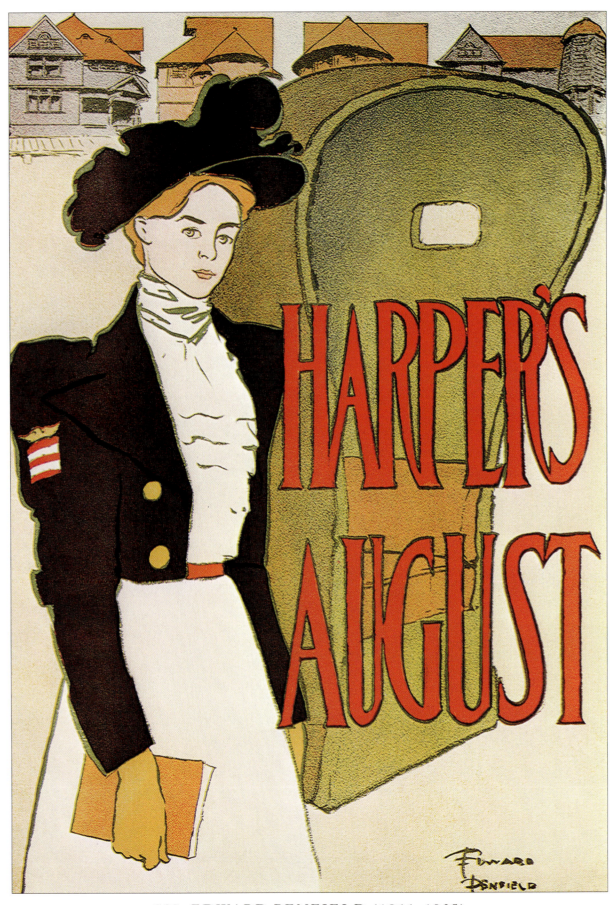

028. EDWARD PENFIELD (1866–1925)
Harper's August, 1897
13¼ x 18½ in. (33.6 x 46.9 cm)

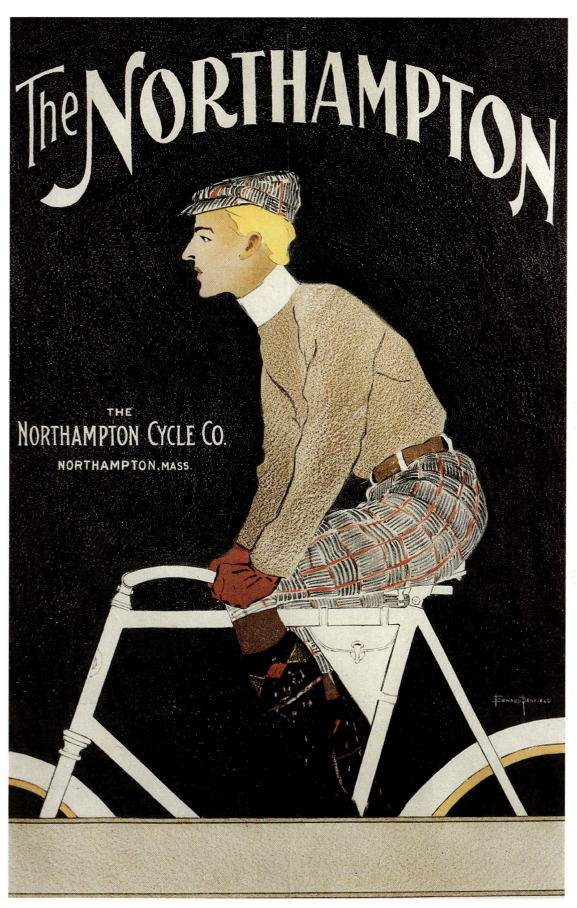

029. EDWARD PENFIELD (1866–1925)
Northampton Cycle, ca. 1899
40 x 26¼ in. (101.5 x 67 cm)

030. EDWARD PENFIELD (1866–1925)
Harper's June, 1896
18¾ x 13¾ in. (47.8 x 34.9 cm)

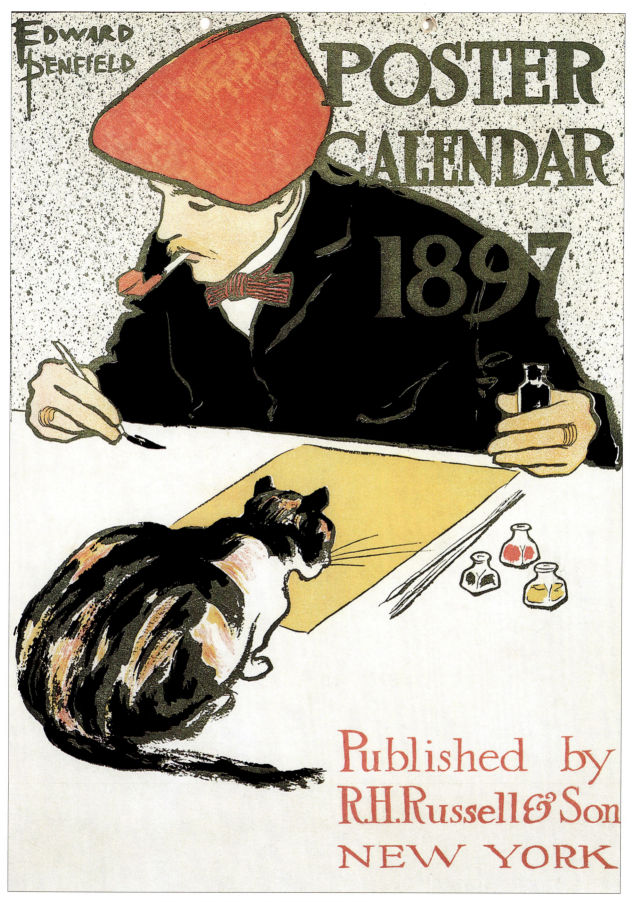

031. EDWARD PENFIELD (1866–1925)
Poster Calendar, 1897
14 x 10¼ in. (35.5 x 25.8 cm)

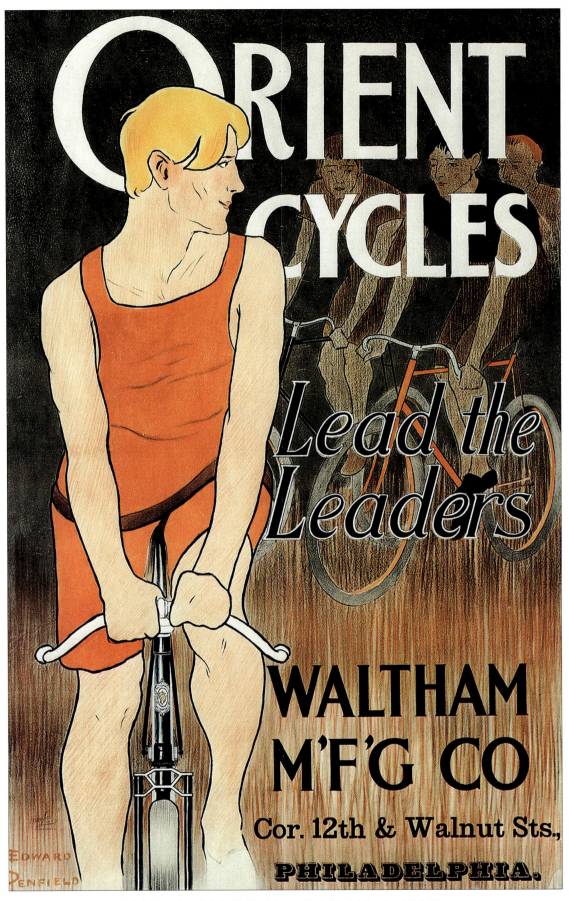

032. EDWARD PENFIELD (1866–1925)
Orient Cycles, ca. 1895–96
39⅞ x 26⅛ in. (101.3 x 66.3 cm)

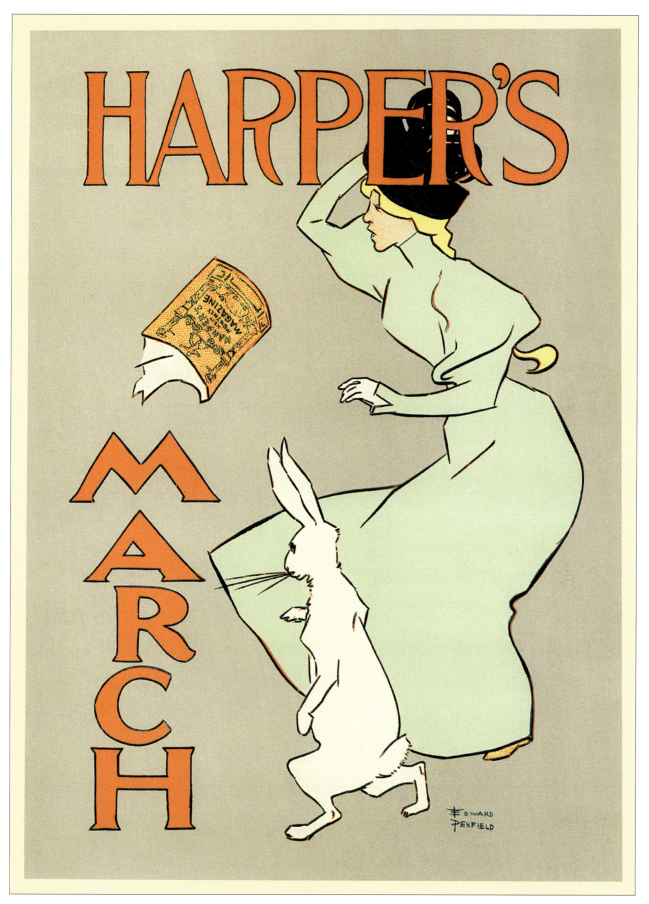

033. EDWARD PENFIELD (1866–1925)
Harper's March, 1894
19½ x 14 in. (49 x 35 cm)

034. EDWARD PENFIELD (1866–1925)
Harper's May, 1896
17¾ x 11⅞ in. (45.1 x 30.2 cm)

035. EDWARD PENFIELD (1866–1925)
Harper's April, 1895
17⅞ x 12¾ in. (45.4 x 32.3 cm)

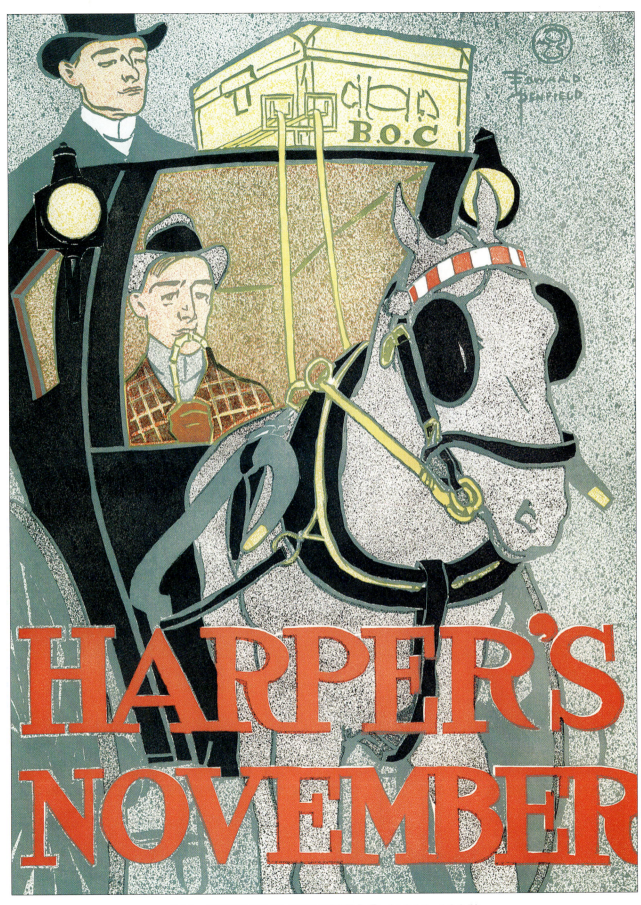

036. EDWARD PENFIELD (1866–1925)
Harper's November, 1896
17¾ x 13⅜ in. (45 x 33.9 cm)

037. EDWARD PENFIELD (1866–1925)
Stearns Bicycle, 1896
53⅞ x 40¼ in. (136.9 x 102.3 cm)

038. EDWARD PENFIELD (1866–1925)
January, February, March, 1897
14⅜ x 10¼ in. (36 x 26 cm)

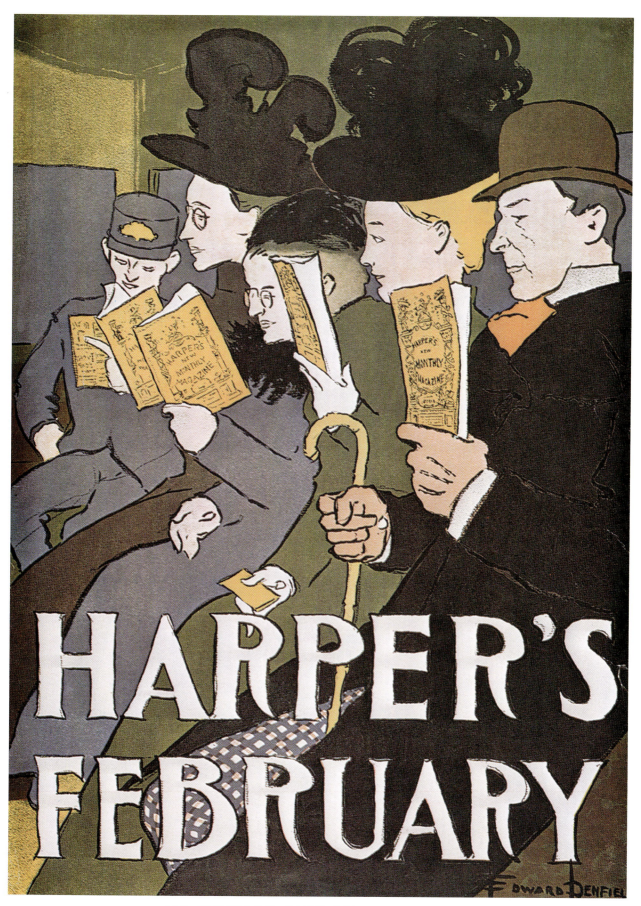

039. EDWARD PENFIELD (1866–1925)
Harper's February, 1897
19 x 14 in. (48.3 x 35.5 cm)

TOM SAWYER DETECTIVE a new story by MARK TWAIN begins in this number

HARPER'S AUGUST

040. EDWARD PENFIELD (1866–1925)
Harper's August, 1896
18⅝ x 13⅝ in. (47.5 x 35 cm)

041. EDWARD HENRY POTTHAST (1857–1927)
The Century, 1896
20⅛ x 14⅛ in. (51 x 35.7 cm)

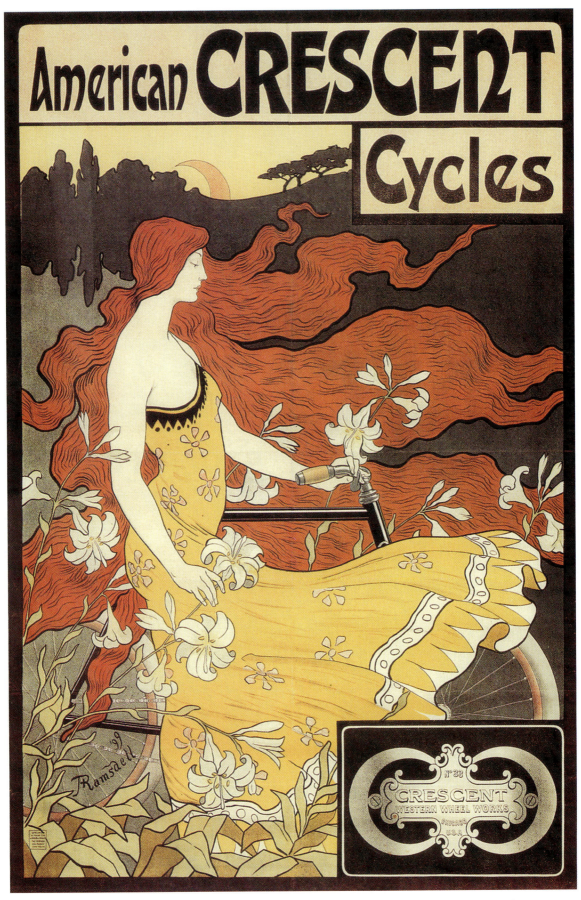

042. FREDERICK WINTHROP RAMSDELL (1865–1915)
American Crescent Cycles, 1899
65 x 44 in. (165.1 x 111.8 cm)

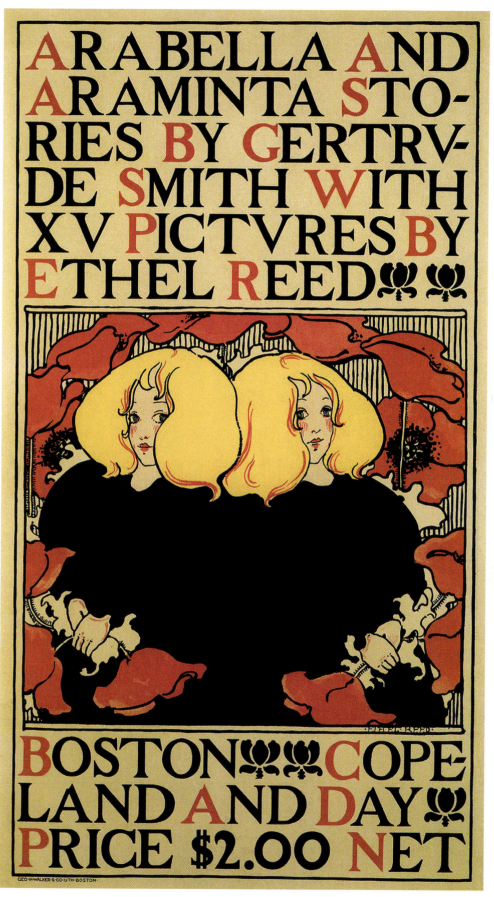

043. ETHEL REED (1874–?)
Arabella and Araminta, 1895
26⅛ x 14½ in. (66.4 x 36.9 cm)

044. ETHEL REED (1874–?)
Miss Träumerei, 1895
22 x 14 in. (56 x 35 cm)

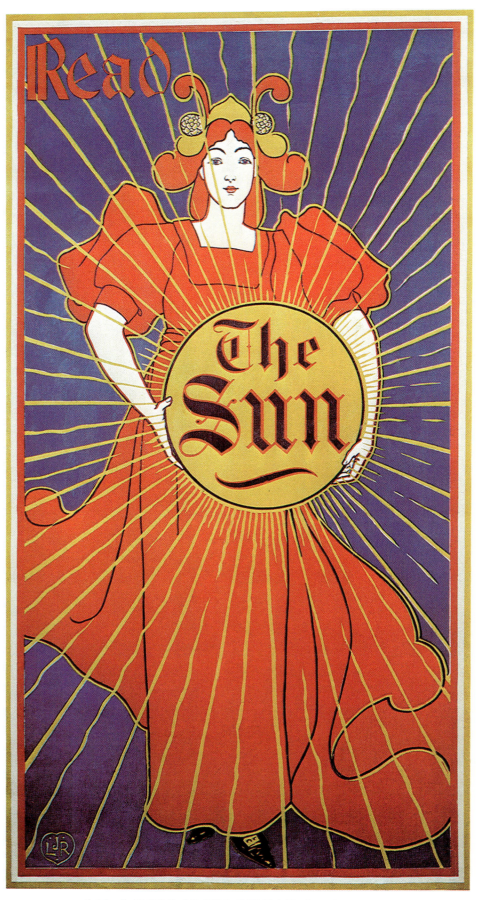

045. LOUIS JOHN RHEAD (1858–1926)
The New York Sun, 1895
42¾ x 23⅛ in. (108.8 x 58.7 cm)

046. LOUIS JOHN RHEAD (1858–1926)
Lundborg's Perfumes, 1894
17¼ x 11½ in. (43.9 x 29.3 cm)

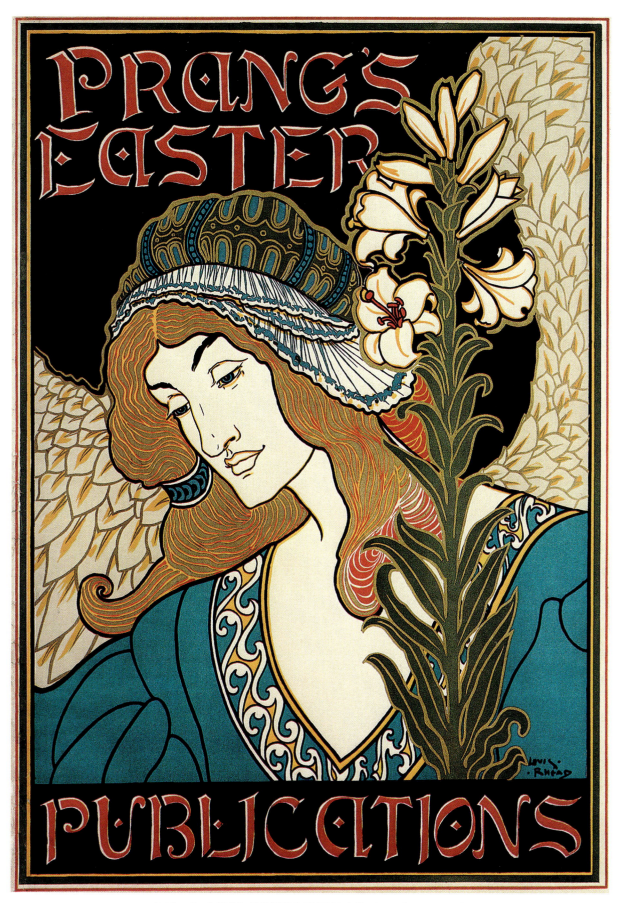

047. LOUIS JOHN RHEAD (1858–1926)
Prang's Easter, 1895
23¼ x 16⅜ in. (57.2 x 41.7 cm)

048. LOUIS JOHN RHEAD (1858–1926)
Read the Sun, 1895
46¾ x 29 in. (118.9 x 73.7 cm)

049. LOUIS JOHN RHEAD (1858–1926)
Salon des Cent, 1897
23⅞ x 16⅛ in. (60.6 x 40.7 cm)

050. LOUIS JOHN RHEAD (1858–1926)
Poster Calendar, 1897
19¼ x 13¾ in. (48.8 x 35 cm)

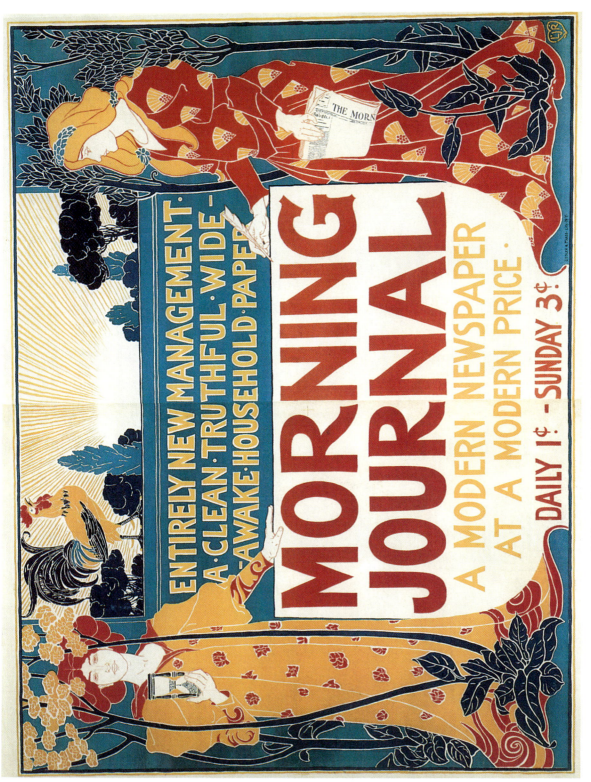

051. LOUIS JOHN RHEAD (1858–1926)
Morning Journal, 1895
17½ x 45 in. (115 x 145 cm)

052. LOUIS JOHN RHEAD (1858–1926)
Scribners for Christmas, 1895
17⅛ x 9¼ in. (43.6 x 24.9 cm)

053. LOUIS JOHN RHEAD (1858–1926)
The Quarter Latin, 1898–99
19¾ x 13⅞ in. (50.4 x 35.3 cm)

054. LOUIS JOHN RHEAD (1858–1926)
His Lordship, 1896
45½ x 26½ in. (115.4 x 67.6 cm)

055. M. LOUISE STOWELL (1861–1930)
At the Sign of the "Old Book Man," 1896
25 x 17 in. (64 x 43 cm)

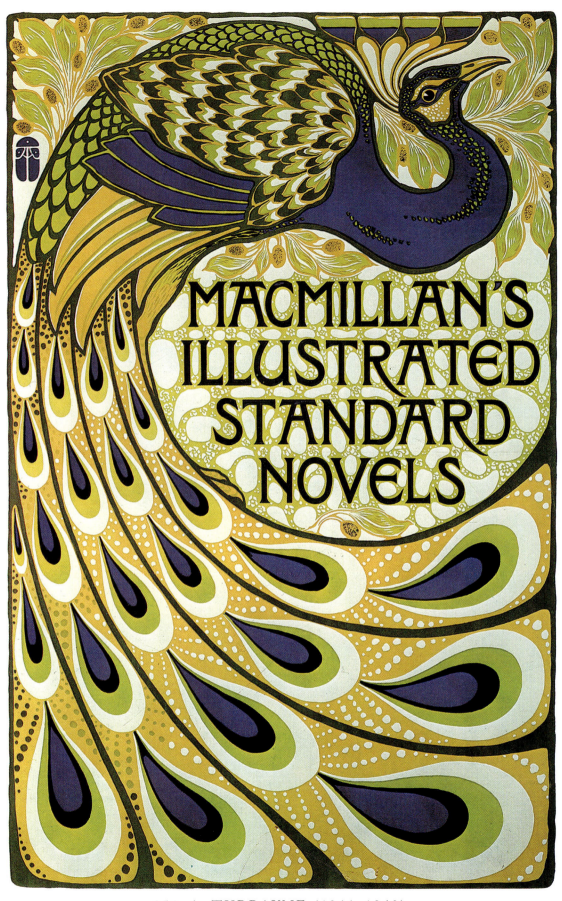

056. A. TURBAYNE (1866–1940)
Peacock Edition, "Macmillan's Illustrated Standard Novels," 1896
34⅛ x 22½ in. (87.8 x 57.1 cm)

057. JOHN HENRY TWACHTMAN (1853–1902)
The Damnation of Theron Ware (or Illumination), 1896
21 x 13 in. (53.3 x 33 cm)

058. IRENE WEIR (1862–1944)
Opera Stories, 1896
28¼ x 14 in. (71.7 x 35.5 cm)

059. CHARLES H. WOODBURY (1864–1940)
The July Century, 1895
19 x 12 in. (48 x 30 cm)

060. UNKNOWN ARTIST
Cincinnati Fall Festival, 1903
40½ x 84 in. (102.8 x 213.3 cm)

BIOGRAPHIES OF THE ARTISTS

Elisha Brown Bird (1867–1943). Bonus image 1. After graduating from MIT as an architect, he chose to pursue a career as an artist creating book plates, advertisements, and posters. He preferred to have his work reproduced by the new printing techniques, rather than having it redrawn by staff artists.

William H. Bradley (1868–1962). Plates 001–012, Bonus image 2. This prolific artist, illustrator, publisher, and printer was often referred to as the "American Beardsley." His style was an offshoot of Art Nouveau, influenced by the Arts and Crafts Movement and Japanese block printing.

William L. Carqueville (1871–1946). Plates 013–016, Bonus image 3. He lived in Chicago for most of his life and designed posters for *Lippincott's* as well as other magazines. He was greatly influenced by the style of Penfield.

Charles Arthur Cox (1829–1901). Plate 017. He was born in Liverpool, England and moved to America. Some of his works included posters for *The Bearings* magazine, published by the Cycling Authority of America.

Arthur Wesley Dow (1857–1922). Plates 018, 019. He was a painter, printmaker, and an art teacher. He studied in Boston and Paris and was the curator of Japanese art for the Museum of Fine Arts in Boston.

Alice Russell Glenny (1858–1924). Plate 020, Bonus image 4. This painter and sculptor studied in New York and Paris. She specialized in murals and only created two posters during her career.

Joseph J. Gould, Jr. (1880–1935). Plate 021, Bonus image 5. This illustrator and designer studied at the Pennsylvania Academy of the Fine Arts. He succeeded Carqueville as a poster designer for *Lippincott's*.

Frank Hazenplug (1873–1931). Plate 022. This illustrator and designer worked mostly for Stone & Kimball who were the owners of *The Chap-Book*, an in-house magazine.

Joseph Christian Leyendecker (1874–1951). Plate 023. This German-born artist moved to America as a young boy. He was a designer of magazine covers, advertisements, and posters. In 1896, Leyendecker won first prize in *The Century* poster contest, which brought him many commissions.

Will Hicok Low (1853–1932). Plate 024. He was a figure and genre painter who studied in Paris with Gérôme and Carolus Duran. He was also an active book illustrator and a poster designer.

Blanche McManus (1870–1929). Plate 025. Bonus image 6. This artist was born in Louisiana and lived in Paris most of her life. She was a proficient author and illustrator for three different book publishers.

Maxfield Parrish (1870–1966). Plates 026, 027. He was a book and magazine illustrator, a poster designer, and a painter of figures and landscapes. Parrish was a student under Howard Pyle.

Edward Penfield (1866–1925). Plates 028–040, Bonus image 7. He was one of America's most famous poster artists. Penfield was an art director at *Harper's* and produced a series of posters to advertise the magazine.

Edward Henry Potthast (1857–1927). Plate 041. Best known as the painter of the summer seashore, Potthast also designed several posters for *The Century Cook Book* and *Metropolitan Magazine*. In 1896 he won honorable mention in *The Century* poster contest.

Frederick Winthrop Ramsdell (1865–1915). Plate 042. This American artist studied at the Art Students League of New York and was a member of the Lyme Art Association between 1907 and 1915. He is best known for his American Crescent Cycles poster.

Ethel Reed (1874–?). Plates 043, 044, Bonus image 8. Best known as a book illustrator, this self-taught artist from Boston emerged as one of the leading poster designers of the late nineteenth century.

Louis John Rhead (1858–1926). Plates 045–054, Bonus image 9. Influenced by Grasset, this English-born artist moved to the United States in 1883 to become one of the most popular poster designers of the late nineteenth century.

Julius A. Schweinfurth (1858–1931). Bonus image 10. This Boston architect was also an artist who created etchings, watercolors, and other graphic designs. He only designed two posters: one for the Boston Festival Orchestra and one for the novel *Quo Vadis*.

M. Louise Stowell (1861–1930). Plate 055. She studied at the Art Students League of New York and with Arthur W. Dow. Stowell created designs for posters, illustrated books, and painted murals. Her specialty was watercolors.

A. Turbayne (1866–1940). Plate 056. Born in Massachusetts, this American artist was a book designer and bookbinder. In 1900 he won third place at the Exposition Universelle in Paris for one of his designs.

John Henry Twachtman (1853–1902). Plate 057. He was one of the first American Impressionists. Twachtman studied painting in Cincinnati and Europe and is best-known for his landscapes. The poster shown is for a novel.

Irene Weir (1862–1944). Plate 058. This author and artist studied at the Yale School of Fine Arts and at the École des Beaux Arts Américaine in Fontainebleau.

Charles H. Woodbury (1864–1940). Plate 059. He was an M.I.T. graduate who studied painting in Paris and specialized in seascapes. Woodbury also designed posters and wrote several books.

ALPHABETICAL LIST OF WORKS

1

BONUS IMAGES

See the link in the "Info" folder on the DVD
to download your bonus images.

6

1. ELISHA BROWN BIRD (1867–1943)
The Poster, 1896
16½ x 10¾ in. (42 x 27.4 cm)

2. WILLIAM H. BRADLEY (1868–1962)
The Echo, 1895
21¼ x 14½ in. (53.9 x 36.8 cm)

2

3. WILLIAM L. CARQUEVILLE
(1871–1946)
Lippencott's February, 1896
19 x 12½ in. (48.2 x 31.7 cm)

7

4. ALICE RUSSELL GLENNY
(1858–1924)
Buffalo Fine Arts Academy and Society, 1897
13⅜ x 8½ in. (33 x 21.5 cm)

3

5. JOSEPH J. GOULD, JR.
(1880–1935)
Lippencott's February, 1897
19 x 11⅛ in. (48.3 x 28.4 cm)

8

6. BLANCHE McMANUS (1870–1929)
The True Mother Goose, 1896
20⅜ x 14¼ in. (51.7 x 36.1 cm)

7. EDWARD PENFIELD (1866–1925)
Harper's October, 1897
19¼ x 14⅛ in. (48.7 x 35.9 cm)

4

8. ETHEL REED (1874–?)
In Childhood's Country, 1896
25⅛ x 11⅜ in. (63.7 x 28.9 cm)

9

9. LOUIS JOHN RHEAD (1858–1926)
Advertising in the Sun Gives Best Results, 1894
45½ x 30 in. (116 x 76 cm)

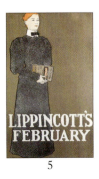

5

10. JULIUS A. SCHWEINFURTH
(1858–1931)
Quo Vadis, 1897
28⅝ x 19¾ in. (72.7 x 50.1 cm)

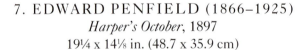

10